Umbra Elysian

Andrew Lehmann

BookLeaf
Publishing

Presentation by *BookLeaf Publishing*

Web: www.bookleafpub.com

E-mail: info@bookleafpub.com

ISBN: 9789358369526

First edition 2023

To M and to M. My rock and anchor.

Thank you for everything.

When My Time Comes

Lay me down so that I may finally rest
A world lacking all of the best
Lay me down when I close my eyes
No more masking this pitiful guise
Lay me down ever so gentle
My fate never grew to be monumental
Lay me down near a bed of flowers
Giving the dirt a new soul to devour
Lay me down when I can no longer stand
Please you can let go of my hand
Lay me down for my next destination
Destined to rest in eternal damnation

Boy Not A Man

A time may come where I fail; written for a later
tale
The story of a boy with dreams who dared to
scheme
He was raised in a world all dreary made by
those weary
In times of desperate measures, death was the
only pleasure
Walking the veil between life and death, on the
brink of his last breath
The boy stumbled from grace trying to find his
place
Slowly drained of a soul, hell would be a happy
stroll

Reflection

I lay awake at night
Torn between what is right
The darkness obscures my light

Quiet storms rage deep inside
Ruined and slain by pride
Thine own Jekyll and Hyde

The fires rage with passion
But I leave trails burnt ashen
Dormant heart lusting with compassion

I fear nothing and only me
Invisible chains desperate to be free
Just one quiet moment I can see

Always fighting the unseen war
With cold hands grasping at the door
The demon awakening at my core

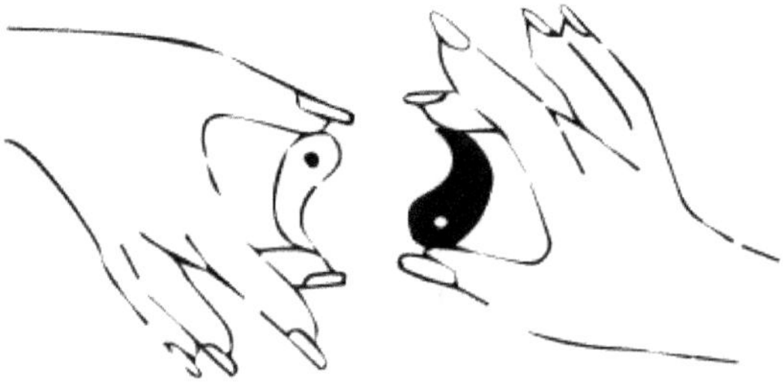

Longing Desire

I can only wish
For love to nourish
As time may pass
The feelings still amass
My heart will beat
With fiery blue heat
Eyes desired from afar
Lighting up my stars
Forbidden fruit tastes sweet
My life remains incomplete

The Demon Within

I struggle to feel every waking hour
All that I have known being devoured

A soul fallen to depths of despair
My mind grew becoming all too aware

What others call insanity is my dream
To pull away from my own seraphim

Welling up with a lifetime of pain
My inner monster shall choose to remain

Fires engulfed me but I found peace
A chaos that needed to be unleashed

From my suffering there is no savior
Others will see fruits from their failures

When you see the bloody red sky
You know the time of my demise

Life to Death

Set me free from this torment I beg thee

A glowering light cast down to Hell's delight

Locked inside my head with thoughts I dread

Beg and beg with remorse but nothing forced

Saints gazing in crudity biased with thine impunity

Allow me to flower my eyes with respiteful guise

Whispered gasps attempt to escape till dawn be reshaped

Solemn steps in silence held with arms in rigid defiance

Filled with dread slowly wrapping the head

As the noose tightens and creaks finally allowed to speak

Eternal passion

A love like mine is worth the world

But pained and scattered through time

The rage, malice, and woes unfurled

A desire to give you the universe being my crime

The Wilt of Time

Let these words say what I cannot speak

For the angel on my shoulder weeps in regret

The devil confident that I am too weak

Withholding a love that I must forget

A garden compiled of wilted flowers

As she waits patiently for infinity

My world slowly darkened and devoured

For her I sacrifice all of heaven's divinity

Grim Hearts

My heart feels still

Slowly surely it kills

Drawing breath this hour

Knowing it may sour

Hoping above it all

To hear that call

Past catching upon me

Ever to be free

Ice cold frozen veins

Legacy hath been stained

A sin upon you

A curse rightly cued

The reaper come due

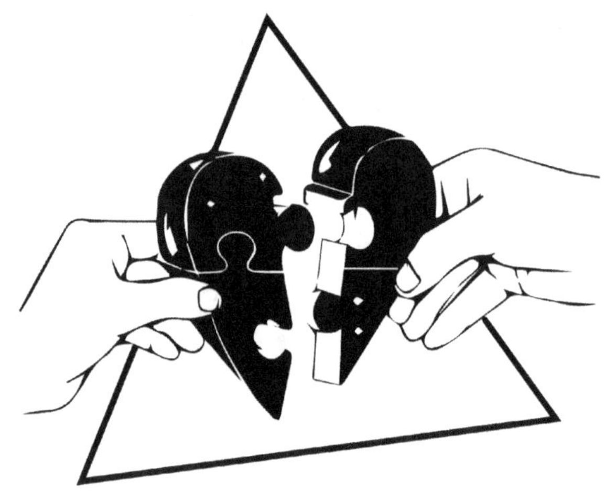

Wounded

War, something that we are all fighting inside

Our homes completely engulfed in divide

The old and rich cowering in luxury away

The rest of giving blood for what we pay

Battle claiming the young and the bold

So the weak in safety may count their gold

Wasting away all that is precious and dear

Every battle fought on a new frontier

While the physical and mental pain is scarred

As the world looks at us in disregard

Peaceless

Time may heal some pain

Black as night, Death I invite

The anger remains

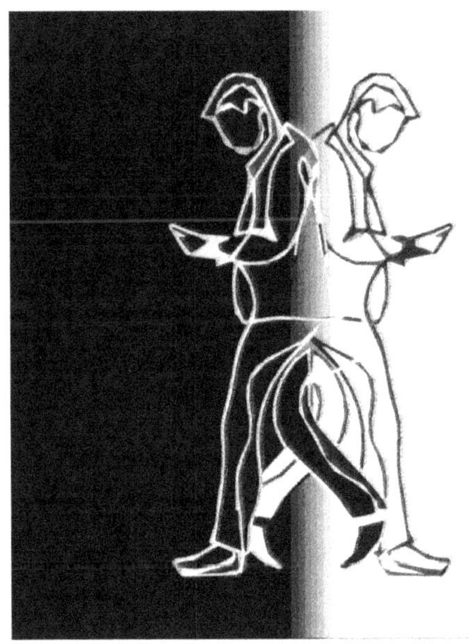

Love Relinquished

A sea of stars separates you from me

My patience still as a tree

We share the same sky and night

Two souls bound for flight

I can only hope and dream

To be worthy of love you deem

The world apart we still must share

Despite all odds I will always care

A bright light shines against the black

Even despite the steel knife in my back

To Depart

My body writhes amongst the masses but not
one eye batted

So-called good souls walking over me lifeless
and vapid

My voice cries for help, drowning in sorrow

As they selfishly only care for their own
tomorrow

My chest beating ready to rip apart and burst

Oh how if the situation were only reversed

My breath raspy as my eyes twitched

The body tangled as if suddenly bewitched

My heart slowly breaking in half falling apart

I hear the bell tolling for me to depart

Locked

This prison of mine

Hidden invisible walls

Trapped in my own mind

Last Breath

Each breath is one second less for living
Every day becoming far less forgiving

Each breath is a day less to spend alive
But not all will see the pearly gates arrive

Each breath is one last memory to treasure
For some life has never had any pleasure

Each breath is one less year to experience
And still our existence may be mysterious

Each breath is one moment closer to the end
Yet some of us never even made a friend

Each breath is a reminder of what remains
Every memory instead holding up more pain

Each breath present not a life but a curse
And death could not make it any worse

My Desolation

All my life I am always the loser
Unloved while everyone else pursues her

I am always alone and to the world unknown

There is no happily ever after in my story
My life reeking and lacking any glory

Betrayed by those dear I beg death to appear

No more soul remains beside a lack of heart
While my life still crumbles and falls apart

No one to call a friend not even to pretend

Without arms that can hold me tight
I shall soon see Hell's demonic light

Drowned Agony

My shadow looms far above
The light dimming and fading
A heart sullen without love

Ensnared deep within my soul
A void seeking to destroy
Fading memories fracture my mind

A final gasp in vain
My heart rotting with pain
What remains is not humane

Reflection

I lay awake at night
Torn between what is right
A darkness obscures my light

Quiet storms rage deep inside
Ruined and slain by pride
My own Jekyll and Hyde

The fire rages with passion
But I leave trails ashen
Dormant heart lusting for compassion

I fear nothing but me
Chained wishing to be free
One quiet moment to see

Always fighting an unseen war
Cold hands grasping my door
Demons awoken at my core

Haiku's Haiku

Words only express

Finesse wordplay for success

Poet's game of chess

Still Here

Pain is the only thing I feel

Pain reminds me that I'm still real

Pain is all that I have ever known

Pain remains especially being alone

Pain reminds me love is weak

Pain is now my willing choice

Pain grows deeper in my voice

Pain shows me all I ever needed

Pain trumps love and succeeded

Pain is just one bad day away

Pain holds the power to end it today

Final Epigraph

Waking up every day is a new regret
To a love that I must forget
When I see what I will never get
Then I know my life is a silhouette

Lost in my mind nay my own head space
Such pity that I forcefully refuse to embrace
All that I love has left me disgraced
If only my heart could simply be erased

A world of people for me to venture alone
Harnessing myself into an unbreakable stone
For my life I will always need to atone
And my soul shall diminish and stay unknown

Now the time has come for a last laugh
As I rip the last piece of my heart in half
The pain remains to breathe on my behalf
A darkness to fully complete my graft

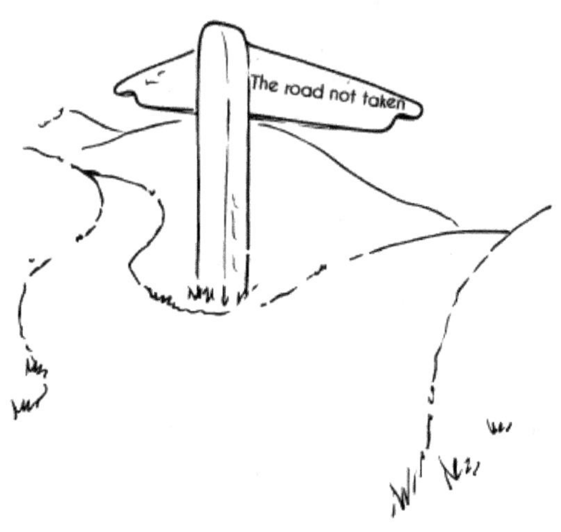

The road not taken

www.ingramcontent.com/pod-product-compliance
Lightning Source LLC
La Vergne TN
LVHW051242200726